Contents

Words that appear in the glossary are printed in bold, **like this**, the first time they occur in the text.

Land at risk

A large part – 71 per cent – of the Earth's surface is covered by oceans while the remaining 29 per cent is land. This land supports a variety of distinctive plant communities like forests, grasslands and deserts. About one-third of the Earth's land is forest. Less than a quarter is grassland and one-fifth is desert. The remaining areas of land are taken up by wilderness areas such as tundra in the Arctic regions and by cities, towns and villages.

This book looks at the problem of **desertification** of land. Desertification is a process in which soil becomes bare and dry, and cannot support vegetation. It can happen very quickly over a few seasons. It takes much longer to bring desertified land back to its original fertile state.

Losing our Earth

About a quarter of the world's land has already been affected by desertification. According to scientists, 24 billion tonnes of fertile soil disappear each year. Over the last two decades, this has added up to an area of land as large as all the farmland in the USA. Desertification removes soil so plants cannot grow. This means that even less water is held in the soil. Animals, plants and humans all suffer from the effects of desertification.

Parched landscape of Tunisia.

Raintree

GREEN ALERT!

Spreading
Deserts

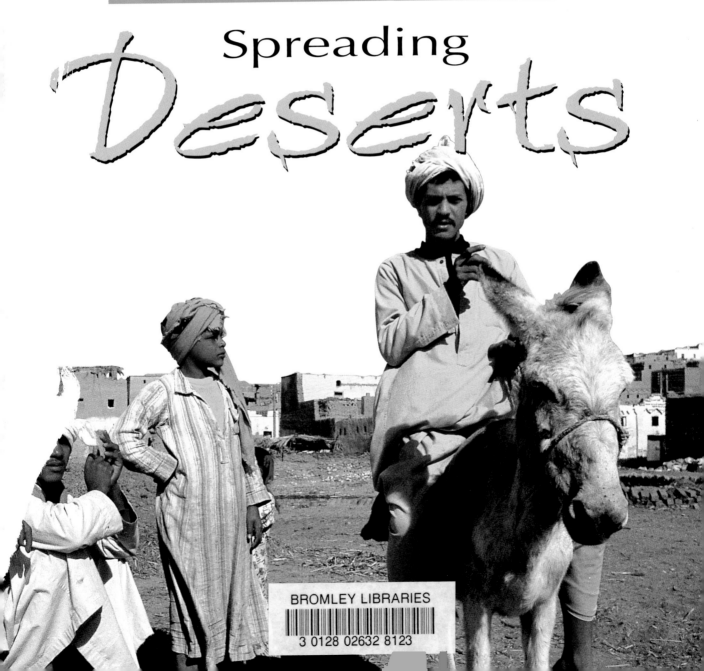

Photo Credits

• Cover: Oliver Bolch (main), Bruce Coleman Collection (top right) • Title page: Bruce Coleman Collection • Imprint page: South American Pictures, Pietro Scozzari, Photodisc, Lonely Planet Images (left to right) • Art Directors & Trip Photo Library: 4, 6, 8, 9 (bottom), 11 (top), 14, 15, 16, 19 (top), 21 (top) • David Simson: 22, 23 (both), 24 (top), 41 (top) • Getty Images/Hulton Archive: 35 (top) • J R Jones: 35 (bottom) • Lonely Planet Images: 7, 11 (bottom), 12, 13 (both), 21 (bottom), 24 (bottom), 25, 26, 27 (right), 29 (centre), 32 (top), 34, 36, 39 (bottom), 41 (bottom), 42, 43 (bottom) • Photodisc: 5 (top), 7 (bottom), 10, 17 (both), 18, 19 (bottom), 28 (both), 45 • Pietro Scozzari: 20, 40 • Science Photo Library: 27 (left), 31 (top), 38, 44 • South American Pictures: 43 (top) • Still Pictures: 29 (top and bottom), 31 (bottom), 32 (bottom), 33, 37, 39 (top and centre) • Topham Picturepoint: 5 (bottom), 9 (top), 30

 www.raintreepublishers.co.uk
Visit our website to find out more information about Raintree books.

To order:
☎ Phone 44 (0) 1865 888113
▤ Send a fax to 44 (0) 1865 314091
▣ Visit the Raintree bookshop at www.raintreepublishers.co.uk
to browse our catalogue and order online.

First published in Great Britain by Raintree Publishers, Halley Court, Jordan Hill, Oxford OX2 8EJ, part of Harcourt Education Ltd. Raintree is a registered trademark of Harcourt Education Ltd.

© 2004 TIMES MEDIA PRIVATE LIMITED
Series originated and designed by
Times Media Private Limited
A member of the Times Publishing Group
1 New Industrial Road, Singapore 536196

Co-ordinating Editor   : Isabel Thomas
Writer   : Paul Rozario
Series Editor   : Katharine Brown
Project Editor   : Lee Mei Lin
Series Designer   : Lynn Chin Nyuk Ling
Series Picture Researchers : Thomas Khoo, Susan Jane Manuel

British Library Cataloguing in Publication Data

Spreading deserts. – (Green alert)
   1. Desertification – Juvenile literature
   333.7'36

   ISBN 1844216659 (hardback)   ISBN 1844216721(paperback)
   08 07 06 05 04   08 07 06 05 04
   10 9 8 7 6 5 4 3 2 1   10 9 8 7 6 5 4 3 2 1

A full catalogue record for this book is available from the British Library.

Printed and bound in Malaysia

Our soil

Soil is the material in which plants grow. It is a very precious resource. The topmost layer of the Earth's surface is covered with soil. On average, soil contains 45 per cent minerals, 25 per cent water, 25 per cent air and 5 per cent **organic matter**, such as decayed plant matter and small animals like earthworms. The most fertile part of the soil is called topsoil. It contains most of the nutrients that plants need to grow. It takes hundreds of years of natural processes to create just a few centimetres of topsoil. Yet, it may take only a few seasons for rain and wind to wash away that topsoil.

Left: This seedling can only grow into a plant if the soil is fertile.

The land degrades

When soil is no longer fertile and able to support plant and animal life, we say that the land has become damaged or degraded. Soil can be damaged by natural forces such as **drought**, strong winds and heavy rain. Human activities also have damaging effects on the soil. People may grow crops or graze animals on the same piece of land for too long. They may introduce harmful chemicals into the soil or use bad farming methods. All these reduce the fertility of the soil. Land degradation takes place all over the world. In the long term, it may destroy the beauty and natural variety of our world.

*A small aeroplane sprays **pesticide** on soya beans to kill pests. Pesticides can seep into the soil and contaminate streams and ponds, affecting fish and small animals that live there.*

A global threat

Across the Earth, 110 countries have land that is at risk from desertification. It affects about 10 million square kilometres (3.9 million square miles) of land in Africa and 14 million square kilometres (5.4 million square miles) of land in Central Asia. North America, some countries of the European Union and the republics of the former Soviet Union all have a serious problem with desertification. In total, desertification has damaged a quarter of the world's land area.

Desertification and the drylands

Parts of the world affected by desertification are called drylands. They include the Sahel and Kalahari regions in Africa, the Great Plains region of the USA and the grasslands of Kazakhstan and other Central Asian countries. Drylands have low, infrequent and unpredictable rainfall. Water is scarce and soils are poor in nutrients. This makes the drylands a very **fragile** environment.

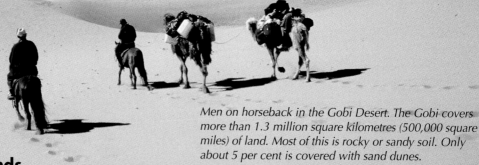

Men on horseback in the Gobi Desert. The Gobi covers more than 1.3 million square kilometres (500,000 square miles) of land. Most of this is rocky or sandy soil. Only about 5 per cent is covered with sand dunes.

Hyper-arid lands

Arid means dry. Hyper-arid regions cover 11 million square kilometres (4.2 million square miles) of land. These regions include real desert areas like the Sahara Desert in Africa and the Gobi Desert in central China. Rainfall in these places is less than 100 millimetres a year. Droughts in hyper-arid lands can last for more than a year. Few animals and plants can survive in these areas. Some people, mostly **nomads**, survive by tending small flocks of animals like sheep and camels. They move constantly in search of the few sources of water in those areas.

Distribution map showing the dry regions of the Earth

Key
▪ Hyper-arid
Arid
Semi-arid
Dry sub-humid

A view of the vastness of South Australia from the Desert Highway.

Arid lands

These areas also have very low rainfall, but they have more rainfall than hyper-arid lands, sometimes as much as 200 millimetres a year. Arid regions include parts of Iran, Iraq, Afghanistan, North America and Australia. Agriculture is possible in arid lands with **irrigation**, using water obtained from rivers and other sources.

*The grasslands of southern Africa are the natural **habitat** of wild animals like zebras, tigers, lions and elephants.*

Aridity of land

The main difference between hyper-arid, arid and semi-arid lands is their level of aridity, or dryness. Aridity is influenced by factors such as rainfall, temperature, wind and evapo-transpiration. Evapo-transpiration is the process by which water returns to the atmosphere as vapour. This can happen by **evaporation** or **transpiration**. Water may evaporate from soil, rivers, lakes and oceans or it may be emitted as water vapour from plants during the process of transpiration. Low rainfall combined with a high rate of evapo-transpiration leads to arid conditions.

Semi-arid and dry sub-humid lands

Semi-arid lands experience either winter or summer rains. In areas that experience winter rains, about 500 millimetres of rain falls every year. A little more rain usually falls in areas that experience summer rains – perhaps 800 millimetres. The Sahel region south of the Sahara Desert in Africa is a semi-arid region. Parts of India, southern Africa and North America are considered to be semi-arid lands. People in semi-arid lands rear cattle and farm the land.

There is more rainfall in dry **sub-humid** lands than in any of the other types of dryland. But the frequency of that rainfall is unpredictable. Dry sub-humid lands include parts of northern and north-eastern China and parts of eastern Europe and Russia.

Natural desert spread and desertification

The word desertification is similar to the word desert. However, desertification is not the same as desert spread. The drylands that are affected by desertification are located in the arid, semi-arid and dry sub-humid parts of the world. Together, these cover about 54 million square kilometres (21 million square miles). The hyper-arid regions of the world are the only real natural deserts.

Natural deserts

Natural deserts, such as the Gobi and Sahara, are caused by climate factors like rainfall, wind currents, air pressure and temperature. These deserts grow and shrink in size according to the climate. This expansion and contraction of desert size can be called desert spread, or the natural growth of deserts. By contrast, desertification is caused mainly by human activities.

However dry they are, natural deserts still support some forms of plant and animal life. These plants and animals have **adapted** over time to cope with the heat and lack of water. Land that has become desertified, however, cannot support plant and animal life. This is another difference between a natural desert and land that has suffered desertification.

Shifting sand dunes of the Sahara Desert in Africa. They stretch from the Atlantic Ocean in the west to the Red Sea in the east.

Importance of the drylands

When scientists study desertification, they concentrate on the arid, semi-arid and dry sub-humid lands. This is because 1.2 billion people, or one-fifth of the world's population, live in dryland regions and are directly affected by desertification. Some of our most important food grains are grown in these regions. These crops include **maize**, wheat, rice and **millet**.

The drylands also support a huge variety of plants and animals. Many of these are found only in the drylands, and nowhere else in the world. The rich **biodiversity** of the drylands is vital to our planet because a diverse community of plants and animals keeps the air and soil clean and healthy.

A wheat field in Kansas, USA.

Climate change or human actions?

Scientists cannot be sure how much desertification is due to climate change and how much is due to human causes. They have, though, found out that the expansion of the Sahara Desert into the Sahel region between 1950 and 1975 was caused by short-term climate changes and not by human activities, which was thought at the time.

It is also possible for desertified lands to support plants again. Many scientists believe that the Sahel region is slowly becoming green again as a result of better land management. Some efforts to reverse the process of desertification are showing good results in many other parts of the world, too.

Desert facts

The largest desert in the world is the Sahara Desert in Africa. It stretches over 8.6 million square kilometres (3.3 million square miles). The longest drought in the last 1000 years occurred in the Atacama Desert of Chile, South America. It did not rain in the town of Calama for 400 years until 1971.The hottest temperature ever recorded was 58 °C (136.4 °F) in the town of Al-Aziziyah in the Sahara Desert of Libya, North Africa. One of the world's driest places is the town of Arica in Chile. Arica, also in the Atacama Desert, receives about 0.8 millimetres of rainfall a year. The picture below is an aerial view of Arica.

Measuring desertification

People measure desertification by studying different types of land such as farmland, as well as areas where no farming is done. They observe how people in these areas interact with the natural world. They take scientific measurements of many things including the level of chemicals in the soil, the number of different species of plant and animal and the productivity of the soil. This information is then used to measure the rate of land degradation and desertification.

Scientists taking samples of soil for analysis.

Observatories

Environmental data on desertification is recorded at **observatories**. One example is the Sahara and Sahel Observatory (OSS) in Tunisia. Here scientists study the Sahara Desert and the Sahel region just south of the desert. They measure changes in the natural resources such as water, air and soil, and look at the impact of human activities on the land.

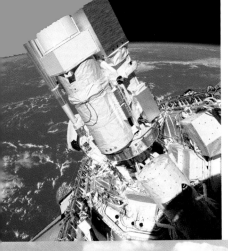

Orbiting satellites

Satellites travelling around the Earth take photographs from a great height. These provide a general overview of the state of vegetation in a particular region. Photographs of the same area taken at intervals of a few years can show whether vegetation is dying or not. These photographs also help to show where forests are being destroyed or replanted.

Sawgrass along the Anhinga Trail in the Everglades National Park, Florida. The Everglades is a biosphere reserve. It is home to a wide variety of plants, animals and wading birds.

Biosphere reserves

The United Nations Educational, Scientific and Cultural Organization (UNESCO) has set up a network of over 400 **biosphere** reserves around the world to record environmental data. These reserves are rich in animal and plant life. Scientists in the reserves study how people interact with the environment and how human activities affect the environment. Some examples of biosphere reserves are the Omo region in Nigeria (Africa), the central Amazon in Brazil (South America), Sierra Gorda in Mexico (South America), Mont Saint Hilaire in Quebec (Canada) and the West Estonian Archipelago (eastern Europe).

Geographic Information Systems

Computers are used to analyze the data that is collected in biosphere reserves, observatories and by orbiting satellites. This data is fed into GIS, or Geographic Information Systems, computers. The GIS present data about all sorts of global environmental factors including drought, rainfall, temperature, water sources, human settlements and road networks. With GIS technology, maps, photographic images and models can be created to predict environmental patterns.

Overcultivation and overgrazing

Overcultivation and overgrazing are two direct causes of desertification. These activities lead to soil **erosion**, land degradation and finally to desertification. One reason for overcultivation and overgrazing is the Earth's rapidly growing human population. In the 1950s, there were fewer than 3 billion people on the planet. By 2000, that number had doubled to 6 billion. With more people to feed, farmers try to grow more food but there is no time to allow the soil to lie **fallow** and build up its nutrients. The land becomes degraded and eventually desertified.

Overcultivation

Cultivation means preparing the land for growing crops. In spite of harsh conditions and unpredictable rainfall, people have been successfully farming in the drylands for thousands of years. They have grown winter wheat, cotton, sugar cane, corn, barley and **sorghum**. However, with the need to grow more food, farmers have been overcultivating the land. Overcultivation means that nutrients are being taken from the soil faster than they can be replaced. The soil becomes less fertile and less productive. Farmers have to plant larger and larger areas just to maintain their harvests. Overcultivation degrades productive land and it becomes desertified.

Harvesting green sugar cane in Queensland, north-eastern Australia. Machines are used to cut off the sugar cane stalks. More than half of Australia's raw sugar is produced in Queensland.

A Fulani nomad with his herd of camels in Niger, Africa.

Overgrazing

The drylands also support another important activity – grazing. Animals grazed by people include cattle, goats, sheep, cows and even camels. Nomadic herders lead their flocks in search of water and to graze on grass, shrubs and small plants. They move on to new areas when the resources in one area are used up. In the past, herders knew just how much time to allow flocks to graze before moving on. Today, though, grasslands are overgrazed. As well as destroying the vegetation, the weight of large herds presses down on the soil, packing it together. This makes it difficult for new vegetation to grow after the herds have moved on. The loss of plant cover exposes the soil to wind and rain, which in turn leads to soil erosion. Land degradation and desertification set in.

Managing grazing

Large numbers of grazing animals can strip the ground bare of vegetation in a very short time. However, studies show that if the land has time to rest, this need not happen. Timing seems to be critical: how long the animals are allowed to graze on the land, and how much time is given for grass to regrow before the animals are brought back on to the land. Some farmers in the eastern state of Oregon, USA, practise timed grazing. In poorer developing countries, herders are often forced to graze their herds on the same piece of land for many months.

A sheep herd in Port Augusta, South Australia.

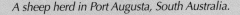

Cattle on Madagascar

The people of southern and central Madagascar, an island off the east coast of Africa, take great care of their cattle because they are a form of wealth and pride. They are given as gifts in business dealings. Even bridegrooms exchange cattle in return for their brides. The problem is that this island has too many cattle. Overgrazing has removed vegetation in many parts of the island. Native plants cannot grow and much soil is lost to erosion. Large areas of Madagascar today are desertified.

Poor farming and irrigation techniques

Poor farming and irrigation techniques can also lead to land degradation and desertification. Today, about 52 million square kilometres (20 million square miles) of drylands are being used for agriculture. About 70 per cent of this **arable** land has already been degraded through the use of bad farming and irrigation techniques.

Monoculture

Monoculture is the continuous cultivation of a single crop on agricultural land for many seasons. It is a farming practice that reduces the fertility of soil over time. Planting the same crop in the same soil for many years also encourages the growth of harmful **bacteria** and **fungi** that attack the roots of plants. They cause the plants to become diseased and die.

Monoculture is practised all over the world. Monoculture crops include both staple crops (such as wheat and maize) that are used for food, and cash crops (such as coffee and tobacco) that are raised for profit. Groundnuts were planted as a monoculture crop for many years in the central and north-western part of Senegal. Today, these areas are no longer productive and suffer from severe desertification. Much of the fertile land of Kazakhstan in Central Asia was turned into cotton fields in the middle of the 20th century. Today, these areas are severely desertified.

Workers packing harvested groundnuts in Senegal. Groundnuts are grown mainly on small farms but this has not stopped Senegal from becoming one of the world's largest exporters of groundnuts.

Intensive agriculture

Intensive agriculture is a farming method that requires large amounts of labour, money and machines relative to the land area. Only one crop is grown, and large amounts of **fertilizer** are used to keep crop **yields** high. Intensive agriculture is practised in many industrialized and developing regions, such as North America and the Middle East. One benefit of intensive agriculture is the doubling of world food production in the past 35 years. However, this has been possible only with a 600 per cent increase in the use of nitrogen-based fertilizers and a 250 per cent increase in the use of phosphate-based ones. Farmers also spray crops with chemicals to kill animal pests and weeds. Over a period of time, these chemicals degrade the soil and contaminate water sources. The degraded soil becomes less and less productive and desertification sets in.

Irrigation techniques

Water can be supplied to crops by diverting rivers, draining lakes and using sprinklers. The amount of irrigated land worldwide has tripled since 1950 to cover 2.7 million square kilometres (1 million square miles). Most of these irrigated lands are in Asia and the Middle East. Irrigated agriculture has helped to double the world's food production in the last 35 years. However, these irrigation systems take precious water away from the land in other places. Lake Chad in Chad (Africa) has shrunk by 95 per cent as the water is drained for elaborate irrigation schemes. Some irrigation techniques also make the soil **waterlogged**. When the water in the soil evaporates, it leaves behind salt, which can poison crops.

Irrigating crops in Luxor, Egypt. Nearly all of Egypt's farmland receives water continuously through modern irrigation systems.

Pesticide poisoning

Some 5 million tonnes of pesticides are used each year all over the world. About three-quarters of this is used by industrialized regions of Europe, North America and Japan. In developing countries that use pesticides, 10 per cent of farmers already suffer from pesticide poisoning. The danger of pesticides is more widespread, however. Pesticides evaporate and pollute the air. The vapours collect high in the atmosphere and then condense in cooler regions of the world. In the Arctic, where the Inuit people live, the pesticides enter the bloodstream of seals and walruses and, in turn, poison the Inuit who hunt these animals for food.

Deforestation

Deforestation is the cutting down of trees for human settlement, agriculture, fuel, animal grazing and commercial **logging**. Deforestation is a direct and major cause of desertification. To understand how deforestation causes desertification, we need to look at the relationship between trees and soils, and how soils are affected when trees are cut down and the **undergrowth** in forests is cleared.

Trees protect soil

There is a very close relationship between soil, trees and plants. Trees and the other plants in forests protect the soil by providing ground cover. The roots of trees and plants hold the soil together and stop it from being eroded away. The soil, in turn, provides nutrients for the trees and plants via the roots.

As well as holding the soil together, plant roots absorb water and minerals that plants need to grow.

No more protection

When trees are cut down and plants removed, the soil has no protection. The tree and plant roots that once held the soil in place are no longer there. This means the soil becomes loose. Heavy rains can wash away the topsoil and nutrients, leaving the remaining earth dry and in very poor condition. Few plants can grow in this degraded soil. Strong winds blow the soil away and desertification quickly follows.

Left: Eroded land. Erosion is a natural process by which rock and soil are broken loose from the Earth's surface. But land is eroded faster through human activities like logging and poor farming methods.

A hard crust

Sometimes a hard crust forms over land that has been cleared of trees and other plants. After a heavy flood has washed away the topsoil, the heat of the Sun causes the surface water to evaporate quickly and a crust forms over the earth. The soil that remains has few nutrients and becomes very dry. The land can no longer support life – it has become desertified.

A section of a cleared forest. Many of the world's forests have been destroyed by fire.

Deforestation for pasture

In Latin America, rainforests are being cleared to create pastures. In Brazil, for example, about 70 per cent of deforestation is to make way for cattle ranches. Cattle grazing usually reduces soil fertility within a few years. People are forced to clear new sections of forest to create more land for the cattle to graze.

Climate change

Climate change can also cause desertification. Drought is a natural climatic event, and it is an important cause of desertification. The climate on our planet is constantly changing. For example, many thousands of years ago, the Sahara Desert was a green and fertile area. However, scientists believe that while climate is an important cause of desertification, human activities can make it worse, especially in areas that are already affected by drought.

Drought

Drought is a period of dry weather caused by a lack of rain for a long period of time over a certain area. The shortage of water affects the soil, plants, animals and people. For example, a serious drought affected the Great Plains region in the USA in the 1930s, and there was a drought in the Sahel region during the 1970s and 1980s. Both these droughts resulted in widespread desertification and destroyed farmland, crops and livestock. In the Sahel, the drought led to famine and loss of human life.

A metal-processing plant in Russia. As well as releasing carbon dioxide and nitrous oxide into the atmosphere, such plants also release lead, a poisonous metal.

The greenhouse effect and global warming

The greenhouse effect is a natural process caused by greenhouse gases in the atmosphere. Greenhouse gases are gases that trap the Sun's heat. The gases include water vapour, carbon dioxide, methane and nitrous oxide. These gases occur naturally.

However, in the last 200 years, the amount of these gases in the atmosphere has increased due to human activities such as burning coal and oil, using nitrogen-based fertilizers and using cars that burn petrol. The greenhouse effect has increased and average global temperatures have risen between 0.3 and 0.6 °C (0.5 and 1 °F) in the 140 years since records began.

Catastrophe!

An increase in temperatures around the world of even a few degrees will cause massive changes in the Earth's climate. A rise in temperature will increase the rate of evapo-transpiration and this, in turn, will lead to a decrease in water and nutrients in soil. The soil will then lose its productivity and become degraded. A rise in temperature can also affect rainfall patterns. Some areas are likely to experience heavy floods while others might experience more drought. This will destroy precious soil, leading to land degradation and desertification.

Global warming also melts ice caps in the polar regions, affecting the animals, like this otter, that live there.

El Niño and La Niña

El Niño is a warm ocean current that reaches the Pacific shores of Peru and Ecuador in South America in late December each year. The current normally lasts for a few weeks. Every three to seven years, however, it persists for many months causing heavy rains, floods and hurricanes around the world. The cooling periods that occur between *El Niños* are known as *La Niñas*, and cause periods of drought.

Desertification and ecosystems

Ecosystems are communities of plants and animals that have a special relationship with their surroundings. Ecosystems link all the **organisms** in a particular area. The soil, air and water on which these organisms depend for life are essential to the ecosystem. If one part of an ecosystem is damaged, other parts are also affected.

Eroded landscape of Loja, Ecuador. Ecuador lies between Colombia and Peru on the west coast of South America. The country cuts across the equator. Hence its name, which is Spanish for equator.

Damage to soil

Soil is a vital part of ecosystems. When soil is damaged, the result is often desertification. Soil can become damaged by erosion from water and wind, which physically remove the fertile topsoil. In the process of erosion, both nutrients and organic matter are lost from the soil. This makes the soil less fertile.

Soil erosion can also be caused by human activities. In the province of Loja in southern Ecuador, years of poor agricultural techniques have left the land very badly eroded. Trees and plants can no longer grow and the ecosystem has become damaged.

An abandoned farm in the Great Plains of North Dakota, USA.

Damage to grasslands

Important grassland ecosystems, such as the **prairie** lands of North America and the **steppe** lands of Russia and Central Asia, suffer from desertification. These areas are covered with long grasses that grow on thick, rich soil. In winter, the grasses hold snow in place. In spring, the roots of the grasses draw the melting water into the soil. Small animals, such as hamsters and earthworms, also help to keep the soil fertile by carrying dead grasses into the soil. Much of these natural grasslands have been destroyed in order to cultivate crops like corn, wheat and barley. These grasslands have been so overcultivated that their ecosystems are under threat. In Canada, for example, about 200,000 square kilometres (77,200 square miles) of prairie land may become desertified through agriculture and animal grazing.

Damage to rainforests

The rainforest is a complex and extremely rich ecosystem that supports many different types of plants and animals. Tropical rainforests are found on and around the equator in Southeast Asia, South America and West Africa. However, the soils of rainforests are thin and they do not contain much organic matter. The richness of the rainforest is stored in the trees. Once the trees in a rainforest are cut down, little fertile soil remains. Farmers who clear these forests find that they can grow crops on this deforested land for up to ten years. Then its fertility is lost. There is also a huge loss of natural wildlife.

This chestnut-mandibled toucan from the Darien Rainforest in Panama may become threatened if its habitat is not protected from logging.

Ecosystems in a rainforest

In an area of only 10 square kilometres (3.8 square miles) of rainforest, there may be as many as 1500 flower species, 750 tree species, 150 butterfly species and countless numbers of mammals, birds and other insects.

CASE STUDY

CASE STUDY
Loss of Mesopotamian marshlands

The region between the Tigris and Euphrates rivers, in modern-day Iraq, was historically called Mesopotamia, or 'land between the rivers' in the ancient Greek language. This area is part of the Fertile Crescent, a region of land that stretched from the banks of the River Nile in Egypt to the plains of southern Iraq. The mountains of Armenia form the northern boundary of this Fertile Crescent and the Arabian Desert is its southern boundary.

Shrinking marshlands

The marshlands in southern Iraq were an important part of the ecosystem of Mesopotamia. Marshlands are a type of ecosystem where the ground is waterlogged, often to a few metres in depth. Marshlands usually form at the mouths of rivers and around river **deltas**. The marshlands in Mesopotamia once stretched across an area of 15,000 to 20,000 square kilometres (5791 to 7722 square miles). Today, the marshlands are about one-tenth of their original size and cover less than 1500 to 2000 square kilometres (579 to 772 square miles) of southern Iraq. **Environmentalists** believe that the last remaining marshlands could disappear in the next five to ten years.

The marsh village of Sarhat in southern Iraq.

Species at risk

The Mesopotamian marshlands were once rich in plant and animal life. The regular flooding of the Tigris and Euphrates rivers produced fertile lands where crops were grown to feed great empires for thousands of years. The area was home to some 40 species of **waterfowl** and it was an important breeding ground for migratory birds from other parts of the world. Mammals unique to the region, like the smooth-coated otter, are now **extinct**. Fishing stocks in the northern Persian Gulf that depend on the marshlands for their spawning cycles have also been severely depleted.

A Marsh Arab gathers **reeds**. *The reeds are used for building homes or for weaving baskets. The marshes provide fish for food and a place for water buffalo to graze.*

Draining the rivers

Why did the marshlands shrink? The reason is that water from the Tigris and Euphrates rivers was diverted from its normal flow via canals and ditches. Dams were also constructed on the rivers to store water. This water was then carried in canals on to the fields of crops. Over a period of 40 years, more than 30 dams were constructed along both rivers. As a result, the marshlands have literally dried up and an entire ecosystem has been destroyed.

A lost people

The people who live in these marshlands are known as the Marsh Arabs or *madan*, as they call themselves. They have also been displaced by the destruction of the marshlands. The *madan* have lived in the marshlands for over 5000 years. Over this long period of time, they learned to live in harmony with their environment. They built their homes on floating islands, all constructed of reeds. Today, very few *madan* still live in the marshlands. Those who do cannot now practise their ancient way of life because the marshland environment has dried up and become desertified.

Desertification and plant biodiversity

The word biodiversity is a shortened version of the phrase biological diversity. Biodiversity refers to the number of different plant and animal species in a particular environment. People who care about our planet now talk about preserving ecosystems in order to maintain the Earth's rich plant biodiversity. Desertification reduces plant biodiversity.

Cacti near Lima, Peru.

A universe in the soil

You may not think there is much life in the soil. On the contrary: almost all major groups of animals have species that live in fertile soil. For example, there may be as many as 10,000 roundworms living within a single cubic centimetre of prairie soil. Organisms that live in the soil help to recycle dead or decaying organic material. Fungi, tiny plants, bacteria and **actinomycetes** maintain ecosystems by breaking down the material into even smaller parts. Depending on the type of soil, climate and terrain, other small animals add to the biodiversity of the soil. These include ants, termites and earthworms. Desertification can harm all this life in the soil, reducing soil productivity and plant biodiversity.

Army ants attacking a butterfly. Ants help to loosen the soil and decompose plant and animal matter.

A green kingdom in the drylands

The drylands support a great variety of different plants, trees and shrubs. These include **lichens**, cacti, grasses and dry forests. Lichens and cacti are hardy plants found in the arid deserts and mountains of North America and other drylands around the world. The grasslands of the Central Asian steppes and the North American prairies support many species of long, short and medium-sized grasses, such as blue grama and buffalo grass, sagebrush and rare species of plant. Savanna grasslands in the drylands of Africa and Australia receive a bit more rain than the prairies and steppes, so they can support trees as well as grasses. Baobab and acacia trees, for example, are well suited to withstand hot and dry conditions.

A man walks on 'Baobab Alley' near Morondava, west Madagascar. The baobab trees are specially suited to dry conditions. The swollen trunk stores water. Almost all parts – trunk, fruit and leaves – can be eaten. They are sometimes called 'upside down trees' because of their unusual root-like branches.

Forests under threat

Desertification reduces plant biodiversity by killing off many plants and leaving only the hardy to survive. Desertification happens so quickly – sometimes in the space of a few years – that plants may not be able to adapt quickly enough to the harsher conditions and they die. The dry forests of western Madagascar is an example of a dryland environment that is being threatened by desertification. These forests receive rain for only a short period each year. They support several rare species of plant. For example, there are seven different species of baobab tree here, compared with just one baobab species in the whole of the African continent. Desertification caused by climate and human activities will threaten this rich plant biodiversity.

Desertification in Tajikistan

A type of plant called teresken grows in the eastern Pamir Mountains of Tajikistan in Central Asia. In recent times, poverty has driven the local people to harvest this plant for fuel. Teresken plants help keep the soil in place on the mountain slopes. Without the plants, the soil has been eroded and many other more fragile plants that grow together with the teresken plants can no longer survive. Desertification has set in as people cut down the teresken plants. As a result, the remaining plant biodiversity in the region is also being destroyed.

Growing olives

Desertification in the Mediterranean region has been a problem for hundreds of years. One area where desertification has set in is the hilly province of Andalucia, in southern Spain, where olives are traditionally grown. Environmentalists believe the cause is a combination of factors – the dry climate, traditional olive growing techniques and the use of machines. Together, these factors contribute to a loss of more than 80 tonnes of soil per 10,000 square metres each year.

Drought and heavy rain

In Andalucia, most olive trees are planted on steep slopes. In most years, there is a summer of drought followed by heavy rains that wash topsoil down the slopes. A hard surface forms after the water has evaporated. This hard crust does not allow water to seep into the soil and reduces the nutrients in the soil. Farmers **plough** the hard ground to plant olive trees but the ploughing breaks up the crust and further destroys the structure of the soil. More soil is washed away by the next heavy rains.

Aerial view of olive fields near Cazorla-Jaen province in Andalucia, Spain.

An olive grove in Andalucia (left) lushly covered with low-lying plants. The nets are placed to catch falling olives and to prevent small animals from eating them. The removal of ground vegetation in another olive grove in Andalucia (right) exposes the soil to heavy rain and erosion.

Loss of vegetation cover

Vegetation cover allows soil to absorb water and keep it healthy. Many varieties of plants grow naturally in and around the olive orchards. These include crimson clover, hairy vetch, dwarf fan palm, the Indian prickly-pear and aloe plants. Farmers remove all low-lying plants in order to control weeds and to plant more olive trees. But when they remove this ground cover vegetation, they loosen the soil, which increases the rate of soil erosion by water and wind. The loss of soil affects the olive plant and reduces the yield from olive orchards.

Use of machines

Olive farmers in Andalucia, especially those with large orchards, now use machines to increase their olive yields. These machines strip vegetation from the soil to make space for planting more olive trees. As a result, the soil around the trees becomes loose because there is no ground cover to hold it in place. Heavy rains then wash away the soil. The increased use of machines also means that cultivation takes place all year round. The land has very little time to lie fallow and recover.

Animal shelter

Ground cover and low-lying shrubs or plants provide shelter for many different species of small animal. These include rodents, like mice and gerbils, as well as insects like ants, crickets and ladybirds. Ground cover also forms the habitat for many species of small bird, such as sparrows. Soil erosion and desertification caused by olive cultivation threaten these animals because they destroy the vegetation cover that forms their habitat.

Desertification and animals

Animals that live in the drylands have adapted over thousands of years to the harsh conditions of their habitats. But desertification, which can happen in less than twenty years, does not give animals enough time to adapt to the drying land. Desertification destroys their habitats and their sources of food and water. The loss of habitat through desertification is a serious problem. Animals without a home have no protection, no food sources and nowhere to bear their young. This affects breeding and mating cycles and can lead to fewer births.

What is the relationship?

Scientists in different parts of the world are studying the relationships between animal habitats, biodiversity and desertification. They want to find out exactly how desertification affects animal populations, which means the numbers of a particular animal species. In general, desertification seems to take place alongside a decline in animal species. It may or may not play a direct role in the extinction of some animal species.

The lion's survival will be threatened if its sources of drinking water disappear as a result of desertification.

No more food

Scientists have discovered that lands that suffer from desertification may also have declining animal populations. This is because desertification can remove the natural habitats of animals. The Iberian lynx, for example, used to roam all over Spain and Portugal. The main food of the lynx is rabbits. Soil erosion, caused by farming and the expansion of towns and cities, has destroyed the habitats of both rabbits and of the lynx. As a result, there are fewer rabbits for the lynx to eat. The loss of their habitats has also affected the ability of both of these species to reproduce. The Iberian lynx is now an **endangered** species with a population of just 600.

Iberian lynx on the prowl. An adult lynx needs to eat at least one rabbit per day to survive.

No more water

From time to time Australia suffers from drought, which can lead to desertification and loss of habitat. Some major drought episodes occurred in the years 1895–1902, 1914–1915, 1937–1945, 1965–1968 and 1991–1995. Many of these droughts were caused by the *El Niño* phenomenon. Animal populations can be severely affected by drought. The northern hairy-nosed wombat of central Queensland is one such animal. This creature is one of the world's rarest **marsupials**. Drought, together with overgrazing by cattle that were reared for milk and meat, has reduced the habitat of the wombat in Queensland to an area of just 3 square kilometres (1.2 square miles).

This northern hairy-nosed wombat lies safe in its natural habitat in the Epping Forest National Park in Queensland.

The fossa of Madagascar

Madagascar is a large island off the south-eastern coast of Africa. Overgrazing and deforestation have recently caused severe desertification. Many wildlife species, including the lesser yellow bat, the mouse lemur and the fossa *(right)*, are under threat. The fossa, a mammal related to the mongoose, is Madagascar's largest native **predator**. It feeds on small animals like lemurs, rodents, snakes and chickens. The loss of natural habitats through desertification has reduced the fossa population to about 2500 animals.

The Barsa Kelmes Nature Reserve

A beached fishing boat on the Aral Sea. This area used to be a harbour on the Aral Sea where ships could dock.

Barsa Kelmes used to be an island located off the north-western coast of the Aral Sea in Kazakhstan. The name means 'land of no return' in the Russian language. Drainage of the Aral Sea, once the fourth largest lake in the world, and desertification of its coastal areas have turned Barsa Kelmes into a peninsula. A strip of land now connects Barsa Kelmes to the mainland. This is bad news for the wildlife on Barsa Kelmes as they are no longer protected by being isolated.

The nature reserve

A nature reserve was founded in 1939 to protect the wildlife on Barsa Kelmes. It spans about 300 square kilometres (115 square miles). It is home to 203 bird species and more than 50 species of animal, including Persian gazelle, the corsac fox and the kulan, one of the rarest hoofed animals in the world.

Aerial view of the Amu Darya river, which flows into the Aral Sea. It is about 2500 kilometres (1553 miles) long, making it one of Central Asia's largest rivers.

Desertification of the Aral Sea region

The Aral Sea is an inland saltwater lake. It receives water from the Amu Darya and Syr' Darya rivers, but no water flows out of it. For more than 30 years, when Kazakhstan was part of the former Soviet Union, water from the Aral Sea was used to irrigate huge areas of cotton and rice that were grown on the land around the sea. In the 1980s, between 50 and 60 cubic kilometres (12 and 14 cubic miles) of water flowed into the Aral Sea every year. Today, it receives just 2 to 5 cubic kilometres (0.5 to 1.2 cubic miles) a year. The total surface area of the lake has shrunk by 60 per cent.

Impact on wildlife

The drying-up of the Aral Sea and the desertification of its coastal lands mean that the water around the island of Barsa Kelmes has gone. It is now connected to the mainland. The kulan and other animals are free to cross over to the mainland, where they are hunted by people for their skins. About 100 kulan still live on the nature reserve but their survival is at risk. The waters of the Aral Sea are also becoming more and more salty as it dries up. This affects the plants that form the habitat of the kulan and other animals of the Barsa Kelmes Nature Reserve.

The kulan

The kulan is a close relative of the horse family but is smaller than the domesticated horse. It can run at speeds of up to 70 kilometres (44 miles) per hour. These animals once roamed the steppes of Central Asia but nearly became extinct as a result of hunting by poachers and the destruction of their steppe habitats. By 1941, fewer than 200 kulan remained in Kazakhstan. In an attempt to save the species, Russian scientists transferred fourteen kulan to Barsa Kelmes. The isolation of the island helped the population of kulan to grow.

Desertification and people

Desertification affects human society in a complex way. Areas that are severely desertified are poor and undeveloped. The people are malnourished. Desertification leads to poverty, and poverty drives people to **overexploit** the remaining natural resources in their environment. Such action only increases desertification and causes yet more poverty. So poverty is both a cause and a result of desertification. Desertification affects the lives of nearly 1.2 billion people on the Earth.

Less food for the people

Desertification causes crops to fail. In the semi-arid Sahel region in central Africa, for example, national food production rose by an average of 1.8 per cent a year between 1961 and 1992. This figure is lower than the average annual population growth in the same area for the same period. This means that there is not enough food for the people. Food has to be imported, usually in the form of food aid and donations. In the long term, though, food aid actually prevents the development of agriculture because it may be more expensive to grow food than to receive it. So food production may decline even further, and food aid may have to be increased to compensate – as in the Sahel.

People in Ethiopia waiting for food to be distributed to them.

Migration to towns and cities

Drought and desertification force rural populations to **migrate**. While some people move to other rural areas that are less affected by desertification, most people try to settle in towns and cities. This puts a strain on those towns and cities. Over the last two decades, about 10 million people in Africa have migrated in search of a better life. The migrants set up flimsy houses on the outskirts of cities. These settlements quickly developed into slums. In just over twenty years, the population of Nouakchott, the capital of Mauritania in north-west Africa, rose from 9 per cent to 41 per cent of the national population, while the proportion of people living in rural areas fell sharply from 73 per cent to 7 per cent.

A slum in Mauritania. Living conditions and hygiene in slums are very poor.

Problems with society and the economy

Desertification can also lead to social problems within a country. When crop production falls because the land is unproductive, there is less money for the government to spend on developing the country. When people migrate to cities because of desertification, they compete with urban dwellers for the little food and water that are available. Hunger, poverty, dissatisfaction and unhappiness can lead to **social unrest** in a country. The United Nations believes that desertification encourages unrest and that it has played a part in several of the armed conflicts that are taking place in the drylands in Africa.

Environmental refugees

Some 25 million people have become **refugees** because of desertification. These people are called environmental refugees. Every day, over 5000 people become environmental refugees. The fishermen in the Aral Sea in Kazakhstan are environmental refugees. They have moved to cities because the desertification of the Aral Sea region and salinization of the water have killed most of the fish – their source of income. The poverty and poor health of these people have been directly linked to the drying-up of the Aral Sea. They are unlikely ever to be able to return to their homelands.

China's dust clouds

Desertification is a major environmental problem in China, the country with the largest population in the world. Sixty per cent of China's population lives in desertified areas. Most of these places are in the north-west part of the country, in the region of Xinjiang. This area stretches for over 1.65 million square kilometres (637,068 square miles) and about 22.5 per cent of this land is desert. The rate of desertification in this region is high. About 3000 square kilometres (1158 square miles) of arable farmland becomes desert each year.

A camel caravan in the Takla Makan Desert in Xinjiang.
The desert is the second largest drifting desert in the world.

Where the wind blows

Desertification in China is mainly caused by deforestation and overexploitation of land for farming and grazing. Extreme drought makes the problem more severe. Strong winds sweep up the desertified earth into huge dust clouds. These winds blow from the Tibetan Plateau in the west and carry the dust clouds hundreds of miles to China's eastern cities and across the sea eastwards to South Korea, North Korea and Japan. These giant dust clouds also blow across the Pacific Ocean and sometimes they can even obscure views of the Rocky Mountains in the USA.

Dust everywhere

The dust clouds are so thick and choking that people in Beijing, the capital of China, need to wear masks when the winds blow in spring. People suffer all sorts of health problems, from asthma to bronchitis and sore eyes. The clouds are so thick that the skies darken. Visibility on roads is reduced and traffic slows down. Schools are shut down. Airports have to be closed and flights cancelled because pilots cannot see through the dust. As desertification in north-western China gets worse, the dust clouds that affect the rest of China become thicker and larger.

Shelterbelts in Xinjiang

To slow down the rate of desertification in Xinjiang, the Chinese government has begun to plant shelterbelts. These consist of green hedges, trees and shrubs that are planted in and around desert oases and farmland to anchor the soil and prevent the wind from blowing it up into dust clouds. Scientists have discovered that a 100-metre wide shelterbelt can stop 90 per cent of sand movement around it. The Chinese government plans to create shelterbelts on over 6300 square kilometres (2430 square miles) of land in Xinjiang.

Right: Chinese women in Beijing protect themselves with silk scarves from strong winds and dust.

Left: These trees were planted to help stop the advance of sand. Only trees that can adapt to arid and sandy environments are planted.

How dust affects our health
Dust clouds are made up of tiny solid particles called particulate matter. This matter can enter the lungs and cause allergic reactions and asthma attacks. People who are sensitive to allergies, or have asthma, experience breathing difficulties. Groups of people who are more sensitive to dust include infants, young children, the elderly and people with a history of heart disease.

International fight against desertification

The United Nations Convention to Combat Desertification (UNCCD) is an international agreement adopted in June 1994 in Paris. To date, 179 countries have signed the convention. The UNCCD is officially called the 'United Nations Convention to Combat Desertification in Countries Experiencing Serious Drought and/or Desertification, Particularly in Africa'. As the long name suggests, the convention aims to help countries that are seriously affected by drought and desertification.

Aims of the Convention

The three main aims of the convention are to increase the productivity of land, restore degraded land and preserve healthy land. Other objectives include encouraging more efficient use of water resources and promoting sustainable development in areas affected by drought and desertification. The idea of sustainable development is to satisfy present human needs for water, land and food without destroying these resources for future generations. So, if someone cuts down a tree, for example, then another tree should be planted to replace it.

A mother and child return home with water for the family. Water is scarce in Africa and the people walk long distances just to collect it.

Children in Burkina Faso queue up to collect water. People here learn about the importance of managing water supply and share that knowledge with the next generation.

National Action Programmes

The convention is implemented through National Action Programmes (NAPs) in various countries and regions. By March 2002, there were 57 NAPs. NAPs specify the practical steps and measures needed to combat desertification. These measures could include promoting research, introducing drought-resistant crops, improving drought warning systems or encouraging farmers to manage their land in a way that supports sustainable development. The most important thing about the NAPs is that they encourage ordinary farmers and villagers to take part and to make decisions, because they are the ones who are directly affected by desertification.

Focus on Africa

The impact of desertification on the environment and on human populations is greatest in Africa. Desert and drylands make up two-thirds of that continent. Three-quarters of the farmland in Africa is already degraded. Many African countries are poor and require a great deal of foreign aid to feed their people. The economy and **infrastructure** of these countries are weak. These problems have been a source of great concern to the international community. This is why the UNCCD, in its official title, makes particular mention of the need to combat desertification in Africa.

National Action Programme in China

In the initial phase (1996–2000), attention was paid to slowing down the speed of desertification by introducing vegetation to degraded lands, building shelterbelts and treating land that is contaminated with salt. Between 2001 and 2010, China aims to improve ecological conditions by planting forests and introducing natural reserves. By the end of the third phase in 2050, nearly all desertified lands in China will be under control.

Conserving water in Algeria

People living in oases in the southern part of Algeria, Africa, have been able to survive extremely harsh conditions by carefully managing scarce water resources, most of which lie underground. These people use an irrigation system that allows them to grow food in a way that protects the environment. Much of this has changed in recent decades because the rapid growth in population and intensive cultivation threaten to dry up the underground reserves of water.

Drying-up of the oases

Many of the oases in Algeria are drying up. The main cause is overcultivation, which uses up precious water resources. The problem is made worse as people give up the traditional methods of water and land management in favour of modern methods. For example, people are digging deeper and using modern pump systems but these pump out far more water than is replaced naturally by rainfall. They are also using a jet watering system to irrigate the land but this allows a lot of water to evaporate. Instead of using animal dung to fertilize the soil, they use chemical fertilizers, which pollute the water.

An oasis in Algeria. Oases are fertile areas in a desert where water is found and plants grow.

The foggara system

The foggara system is a traditional system of water management. It is an important part of Algeria's fight against desertification. Foggaras are underground pipes that were put in place to collect, store and transport water to the surface. The system uses gravity to move water from one place to another. The water collected in this way is organized by a group of community leaders. They decide who gets water, how much they get and what purpose it is to be used for. Some of the foggaras in southern Algeria have been repaired by non-governmental organizations (NGOs). The NGOs also educate the people about the importance of wise water management, planting trees and other ways of combating desertification.

Foggaras are made from a mixture of stone, clay and straw. The water is kept mainly underground to prevent evaporation.

Sustainable use of water resources

The foggara system is in use in many of the world's drylands. It is believed to have originated in Iran some 3000 years ago, where they are called *qanat*. In Morocco, they are known as *rhettaras*. The successful repair and reintroduction of the foggara system in southern Algeria is an excellent model for other oasis communities in the Sahara Desert. Traditional methods of land and water management are therefore very important in helping communities in the drylands to survive in the future.

Another similar form of irrigation in Algeria. This water system was developed centuries ago by the Tuaregs, a nomadic people.

Date palms

People in oasis communities in northern Africa are encouraged to plant date palm trees. The date palm provides dates, which are the main source of food for these people. The trees also supply wood for building and carpentry and fibre for clothes, basketry, furniture and weaving. Sugar, vinegar and alcohol can also be derived from the date palm. Another important reason for planting date palms is that they stop the Saharan sands from shifting into the oases.

Women combat desertification in India

The causes of desertification in India are similar to those in other countries – harmful human activities and a harsh climate. Climatic conditions include drought, unpredictable rainfall, variable temperatures and floods. Harmful human activities include overcultivation, overgrazing, deforestation and poor irrigation methods. India's large population also places a great strain on natural resources such as water and land. When the land is overexploited, the soil loses its productivity and soil erosion occurs.

Coping with infertile land

In India, desertification has had important social and economic consequences. As the land becomes severely degraded, many farmers abandon their fields to find work in the towns. They leave behind female family members who must try to make a living from land that is no longer fertile. It is the women who normally take care of the homes and manage resources such as **livestock**, water and fuel. With the men gone, women also have to tend to the increasingly degraded fields.

This woman weaves baskets to supplement her family income.

A woman works on a fruit farm in Andhra Pradesh, using skills taught by NGOs.

Women at work

Some non-governmental organizations (NGOs) have stepped in to help these women. The NGOs identify women who can organize and lead others. They educate them on the need to combat desertification. With these new skills, the women are able to start small income-generating projects such as planting fruit trees, cultivating vegetables and making baskets. The women also change their farming practices to manage the fields better. They build small dykes, or walls, around the fields to keep rain water on arable land. They also learn to plant trees that are more suitable for dry climates.

A green landscape in Andhra Pradesh

One project in the eastern state of Andhra Pradesh has been particularly successful. Women take up new jobs that reduce the pressure on land and bring in an income. With a little extra money, poverty decreases and fields can lie fallow for longer, so increasing their fertility. The land recovers slowly and becomes green once again. The trees that are planted also supply animal feed, firewood, timber for building houses and fruit for selling or eating. These resources are properly managed by women who have been educated to look after their environment.

Picking mulberry leaves in the countryside of Andhra Pradesh.

Youth For Action

Youth for Action is an Indian NGO that set up the project to help women in the state of Andhra Pradesh. Some 3000 women in 50 villages in the Mahabubnagar district of Andhra Pradesh are now involved in the project. The project is funded by the local and national governments of India and by international aid agencies such as OXFAM and the Rockefeller Foundation.

Global citizens

Desertification is a global phenomenon. It affects over 1.2 billion people living in more than 110 countries around the world. Seventy per cent of the agricultural land in arid, semi-arid and dry sub-humid lands is already degraded. Desertification causes poverty and social, economic and political instability. The United Nations Convention to Combat Desertification (UNCCD) can help us to stop desertification. We must use it to save our planet.

Children unite!

The Recoleta School is a small village school located about 250 kilometres (135 miles) north of Santiago, the capital of Chile, South America. The Recoleta region suffers from serious land degradation caused by overgrazing and overexploitation of the land. All 110 pupils and nine teachers at the school decided to help combat desertification in their neighbourhood. They formed themselves into 'ecological teams'. In these teams, they learned the basics of environmental protection and started a nursery where they use proper farming techniques. Now, they sell their crops and travel to other schools to educate more children about desertification. They show them how to stop its spread by managing the land correctly.

Erosion of farmland in Chile.

The power of traditional knowledge

Indigenous knowledge has been tapped to combat desertification in the slopes of Loja province in the Andes mountains of Ecuador. The elders of the region have great knowledge of the importance of local plants. One of these plants is the nopal tree, or prickly pear, which is a type of cactus. The fruits and leaves are both edible. Now, long lines of nopal trees are being planted to create fences. These fences hold the soil together and stop erosion. The nopal also provides a habitat for the cochineal insect. This insect has been used by Andean people for centuries as a source of red dye for clothing and ceramics. Traditional knowledge has helped stop land degradation and provides a source of nutrition and income for the local people.

Wild nopal cactus. The white spots are cochineal insects.

Cooperation is the key

The UNCCD believes that partnership can help combat desertification. The National Action Programmes formed under the convention involve international, national, governmental, non-governmental and community agencies. In the Cape Verde Islands off the western coast of Africa, volunteers from the United Nations are working with the Cape Verde government to introduce young people to the benefits of combating desertification. The young people are being encouraged to set up pro-environment businesses that protect the fragile ecosystem of the islands. This programme is an excellent example of cooperation between a government, a local community and an international organization.

Sao Nicolau Island, Cape Verde.

In a nutshell

Desertification:

- is caused by climatic factors such as drought, as well as overcultivation, overgrazing, bad farming or irrigation methods and deforestation
- damages soil and makes it infertile for growing crops
- destroys communities of plants and animals
- leads to poverty, famine and ill-health
- encourages social and political unrest.

What can I do?

One way to combat desertification is to read about it. We should educate ourselves about the causes and consequences of desertification and promote awareness of desertification in our community. Remember, 17 June of every year is World Day to Combat Desertification and Drought. Here are some things you can do on the day.

Set up an exhibition on desertification in your school

- Organize an essay competition on desertification and its consequences. Display the best essay at the exhibition.
- Organize a painting competition with the theme 'Desertification and Drought'. Display the paintings.
- Make a large map to show the dry regions of the world. Glue sand on the desert areas and decorate the remaining parts appropriately. Make little national flags and stick these on the countries that suffer from desertification. Display the map at the exhibition.
- Contact the United Nations office in your country and invite a representative to speak about desertification at your exhibition.
- Put up posters to announce the exhibition and invite your friends and family to attend.

Children planting a tree. By learning to take care of plants and the soil, you can help protect the land in your area from being damaged.

This grassland is the habitat for many small animals like rabbits and squirrels. The diversity of living things that can be found here will be lost if desertification sets in.

Establish an environmental monitoring system

- Form ecological teams with your classmates to record the environmental information around you. Decide which factors you want to look at. For example, you could study the weekly water consumption in school, or the amount of paper that is being thrown away, or the number of trees that are being destroyed or planted around your school.
- Make a log book to record all your measurements, week by week, month by month.
- Review the data after a year to see how your local environment is doing.

Start a school garden with a difference

- Choose only plant species that normally grow in your country and are suited to your local soil conditions. Make sure you dig, sow and water the soil in a way that is environmentally friendly.

Ask the experts

- Organize an interview with a local government representative and ask them about the measures that are being taken to conserve environments and animal habitats in your area.
- Invite leaders of environmental NGOs to come to your school to talk about how they combat desertification.
- If your school has a radio service, broadcast these interviews. If your school has its own newspaper or newsletter, print them. Invite students and teachers to give their reactions to these interviews.

Glossary

actinomycetes fungi-like bacteria that help to break down dead plant matter. They form long threads that stretch through the soil.

adapt change or adjust in order to fit new circumstances

arable land suitable for growing crops

bacteria microscopic organisms that have one cell and can cause disease

biodiversity number of different plant and animal species that are present within a given area

biosphere the part of the Earth's soil, water and atmosphere that supports life

delta area of low, flat land where a river splits and spreads out into several branches before entering the sea

desertification process in which soil becomes bare and dry and cannot support vegetation

drought long period when there is no rain

endangered at risk of becoming extinct

environmentalist person who is concerned about the harmful effects of human activity on the environment

erosion loosening and carrying away of rock material by water, wind, animals and even human activity

evaporation process in which a liquid transforms into vapour

extinct no longer exists, dead

fallow period during which farmland is not used to grow crops. This allows the land to rest, and gives time for nutrients to be restored to the soil.

fertilizer chemical substance containing plant nutrients, especially nitrogen, potassium and phosphates. Fertilizers are added to soil to improve the yield and quality of plants.

fragile easily damaged or destroyed

fungus organism that does not have leaves or roots, and lacks chlorophyll to make food. Fungi obtain their nutrients from other living organisms.

habitat part of the environment in which a particular plant or animal normally lives

indigenous belonging naturally to an area

infrastructure permanent services and equipment that are needed for a country to function properly. These include roads, railways, hospitals, schools and power supply.

irrigation supply of water to agricultural land by artificial means such as dams, sprinklers or channels

lichen fungus that grows on rocks, leaves or tree trunks. Lichens obtain their nourishment from the air and spread by producing spores.

livestock animals like cattle, pigs, goats, sheep and poultry that are kept for the production of meat, milk or wool

logging cutting trees and preparing timber

maize plant which produces cobs of sweetcorn

mammal warm-blooded animal that gives birth to live young and suckles its young

marsupial mammal that suckles and carries its young in its pouch. Examples of marsupials are kangaroos, wallabies, koalas and wombats.

migrate move from one place to another, especially to find work or to live

millet cereal which is grown for its seeds or hay

nomad person without a permanent home. Nomads travel from place to place seeking food and pasture for themselves and their animals.

observatory place designed and used for the study of the Earth, the planets and the stars

organic matter material that is made by a living organism

organism any living structure – plant, animal, fungus, bacterium – capable of growth and reproduction

overexploit misuse something to meet one's needs

pesticide any chemical compound that is used to kill pests

plough turn over the surface of the soil

prairie treeless, grass-covered plain (in North America)

predator animal that kills and eats other animals

reed grass that grows in shallow water

refugee person who seeks safety in another country

salinity amount of salt in a body

social unrest disturbance or disorder among people

sorghum cereal which can be made into flour or syrup

steppe dry, grassy and usually treeless plain (from the Ukraine to the Manchurian plains)

sub-humid having lower levels of heat and wetness

transpiration evaporation of water vapour in plants through the leaves

undergrowth thick growth of shrubs and bushes among trees

yield amount of food produced on an area of land

waterfowl bird living on or near water

waterlogged saturated or soaked with water

Finding out more

Books:

Disasters in Nature: Drought, Patience Coster
(Heinemann Library, 2000)

Disasters in Nature: Floods, Patience Coster
(Heinemann Library, 2000)

Earth Files: Deserts, Anita Ganeri
(Heinemann Library, 2003)

Taking Action: Friends of the Earth, Louise Spilbury
(Heinemann Library, 2000)

Videos:

Africa – The Serengeti, National Geographic (1994)

American Deserts, Schlessinger Media (2000)

Desert. Biomes of the World in Action series,
Schlessinger Media (2003)

Earth at Risk – Degradation of the Land,
Schlessinger Media (1993)

Eyewitness – Desert, DK Publishing (1996)

State of the Planet, BBC Natural History Unit (2000)

Websites:

Secretariat of the United Nations Convention to
Combat Desertification
http://www.unccd.int/main.php

Canadian International Development Agency
http://www.acdi-cida.gc.ca/desertification-e.htm

Environmental database for use in schools
(Southampton University, UK)
http://www.soton.ac.uk/~engenvir/environment/
biodiversity/desert.htm

United Nations
http://earthwatch.unep.net/desertification/index.php

Climate Ark
http://www.climateark.org

Global warming.org
http://www.globalwarming.org

Organizations:

Conservation International
1919 M Street
NW Suite 600
Washington, D.C. 20036, USA
Phone: 202 912 1000
http://www.conservation.org

Environment Australia
John Gorton Building
King Edward Terrace
Parkes ACT 2600, Australia
Phone: 61 2 6274 1111
Fax: 61 2 6274 1666
http://www.ea.gov.au

Oxfam Supporter Services Department
Oxfam House
274 Banbury Road
Oxford OX2 7D2, UK
Phone: 44 1865 312610
http://www.oxfam.org.uk

Sierra Club
Headquarters
85 Second Street, 2nd Floor
San Francisco, CA 94105, USA
Phone: 415 9775 500
Fax: 415 9775 799
http://www.sierraclub.org

Disclaimer: All the Internet addresses (URLs) given
in this book were valid at the time of going to press.
However, due to the dynamic nature of the Internet,
some addresses may have changed or sites may have
changed or ceased to exist since publication. While the
author and Publisher regret any inconvenience this may
cause readers, no responsibility for any such changes
can be accepted by either the author or the Publisher.

Index